50 Classic Lazy Gourmet Dishes

By: Kelly Johnson

Table of Contents

- One-Pan Lemon Herb Chicken
- Caprese Avocado Toast
- Baked Brie with Fig Jam
- Creamy Mushroom Risotto
- Garlic Shrimp over Angel Hair
- Truffle Oil Popcorn
- Prosciutto-Wrapped Asparagus
- Burrata with Roasted Tomatoes
- Pesto Zoodle Bowl
- Ricotta Stuffed Shells
- Olive Tapenade Flatbread
- Tomato Basil Soup with Grilled Cheese Croutons
- Crispy Polenta with Parmesan
- Wine-Butter Mussels
- Herbed Goat Cheese Crostini
- Gnocchi with Brown Butter Sage
- Sweet Potato and Feta Hash

- Frittata with Spinach and Leeks
- Lemon Ricotta Pancakes
- Honey Glazed Carrots with Thyme
- Seared Tuna with Sesame Crust
- Soft-Boiled Eggs with Toast Soldiers
- Maple Dijon Roasted Chicken Thighs
- Balsamic Glazed Portobello Mushrooms
- Pan-Fried Halloumi with Grapes
- Roasted Beet and Orange Salad
- Creamy Garlic Parmesan Orzo
- Caramelized Onion Tart
- Herb Crusted Baked Cod
- Arugula Pear Salad with Blue Cheese
- White Wine Garlic Clams
- Shaved Brussels with Lemon and Pecorino
- Buttered Leeks and Poached Egg Toast
- Roasted Red Pepper Pasta
- Mushroom Toast with Gruyère
- Baked Sweet Potato with Tahini Drizzle

- Mediterranean Chickpea Bowl
- Zucchini Fritters with Dill Yogurt
- Roasted Cauliflower Steak
- Artichoke and Spinach Flatbread
- Eggplant Caponata on Sourdough
- Warm Lentil Salad with Dijon Vinaigrette
- Smashed Chickpea Avocado Salad
- Spaghetti Aglio e Olio
- Greek Yogurt with Honey and Pistachios
- Tomato Confit on Baguette
- Baked Eggs in Marinara
- Smoked Salmon and Cream Cheese Bagel
- Chèvre and Roasted Grape Crostini
- Crispy Sage Butter Ravioli

One-Pan Lemon Herb Chicken

Ingredients:

- 2 chicken breasts
- 1 tbsp olive oil
- Juice of 1 lemon
- 2 garlic cloves, minced
- 1 tsp Italian herbs
- Salt, pepper
- Optional: sliced lemon for garnish

Instructions:

1. Sear chicken in olive oil until golden.
2. Add garlic, lemon juice, herbs, and seasonings.
3. Cover and simmer for 10–12 minutes, flipping once.
4. Serve with roasted veggies or rice.

Caprese Avocado Toast

Ingredients:

- 2 slices of toasted sourdough
- 1 avocado, mashed
- Fresh mozzarella slices
- Cherry tomatoes, halved
- Balsamic glaze, fresh basil

Instructions:

1. Spread avocado on toast.
2. Top with mozzarella, tomatoes, basil.
3. Drizzle with balsamic glaze and serve.

Baked Brie with Fig Jam
Ingredients:

- 1 wheel of brie
- 2 tbsp fig jam
- Optional: chopped nuts, puff pastry

Instructions:

1. Place brie on parchment. Top with jam and nuts.
2. Bake at 375°F (190°C) for 10–12 minutes, or wrap in pastry and bake 20 min.
3. Serve with crackers or baguette slices.

Creamy Mushroom Risotto
Ingredients:

- 1 cup arborio rice
- 2 tbsp butter
- 1 small onion, diced
- 2 cups mushrooms, sliced
- 1/4 cup white wine (optional)
- 3–4 cups warm broth
- 1/4 cup Parmesan

Instructions:

1. Sauté onion and mushrooms in butter until tender.
2. Add rice, toast 2 minutes.
3. Stir in wine (if using), then broth 1 ladle at a time.
4. Stir constantly until creamy, finish with Parmesan.

Garlic Shrimp over Angel Hair

Ingredients:

- 1/2 lb shrimp, peeled
- 6 oz angel hair pasta
- 2 tbsp butter
- 3 garlic cloves, minced
- Juice of 1 lemon
- Red pepper flakes, parsley

Instructions:

1. Cook pasta and set aside.
2. Sauté garlic in butter, add shrimp and cook until pink.
3. Add lemon juice, toss with pasta.
4. Top with red pepper and parsley.

Truffle Oil Popcorn

Ingredients:

- 1/3 cup popcorn kernels
- 1 tbsp olive oil
- 1 tsp truffle oil
- Salt, Parmesan (optional)

Instructions:

1. Pop kernels in olive oil over medium heat.
2. Drizzle with truffle oil, toss with salt and cheese.
3. Serve warm for a gourmet snack.

Prosciutto-Wrapped Asparagus
Ingredients:

- 1 bunch asparagus, trimmed
- 6–8 slices prosciutto
- Olive oil, pepper

Instructions:

1. Wrap asparagus spears with prosciutto.
2. Drizzle with olive oil, sprinkle pepper.
3. Roast at 400°F (200°C) for 12–15 minutes.

Burrata with Roasted Tomatoes

Ingredients:

- 1 ball burrata cheese
- 1 cup cherry tomatoes
- 1 tbsp olive oil
- Salt, pepper, balsamic glaze, basil

Instructions:

1. Roast tomatoes with olive oil, salt, pepper at 400°F (200°C) for 15 min.
2. Plate with burrata, drizzle with glaze and basil.

Pesto Zoodle Bowl
Ingredients:

- 2 zucchini, spiralized
- 2 tbsp pesto
- Cherry tomatoes, pine nuts, Parmesan

Instructions:

1. Sauté zoodles in olive oil for 2–3 minutes.
2. Toss with pesto, tomatoes, and pine nuts.
3. Top with shaved Parmesan.

Ricotta Stuffed Shells
Ingredients:

- 12 jumbo pasta shells
- 1 cup ricotta cheese
- 1/2 cup shredded mozzarella
- 1/4 cup grated Parmesan
- 1 egg, salt, pepper
- 1 cup marinara sauce

Instructions:

1. Cook shells al dente.
2. Mix ricotta, mozzarella, Parmesan, egg, salt, pepper.
3. Fill shells, place in baking dish with sauce.
4. Bake at 375°F (190°C) for 25 minutes.

Olive Tapenade Flatbread

Ingredients:

- 1 pre-made flatbread or naan
- 1/3 cup olive tapenade
- 1/4 cup feta or goat cheese crumbles
- Arugula or basil (optional)
- Olive oil drizzle

Instructions:

1. Spread tapenade on flatbread.
2. Sprinkle with cheese.
3. Bake at 400°F (200°C) for 8–10 minutes.
4. Top with fresh greens and a light olive oil drizzle.

Tomato Basil Soup with Grilled Cheese Croutons
Ingredients:

- 1 tbsp olive oil
- 1/2 onion, chopped
- 2 garlic cloves, minced
- 1 can (28 oz) crushed tomatoes
- 1 cup broth
- Handful of fresh basil
- 1/2 cup cream (optional)
- Grilled cheese sandwich, cut into cubes

Instructions:

1. Sauté onion and garlic, then add tomatoes and broth.
2. Simmer 15 minutes, blend with basil and cream.
3. Top with grilled cheese croutons.

Crispy Polenta with Parmesan

Ingredients:

- 1 tube pre-cooked polenta, sliced
- 2 tbsp olive oil
- 1/4 cup grated Parmesan
- Salt, pepper, herbs

Instructions:

1. Pan-fry polenta slices in oil until crispy on both sides.
2. Sprinkle with Parmesan and herbs.
3. Serve warm as an appetizer or side.

Wine-Butter Mussels

Ingredients:

- 2 lbs mussels, cleaned
- 2 tbsp butter
- 3 garlic cloves, minced
- 1/2 cup white wine
- Fresh parsley, lemon wedges

Instructions:

1. Sauté garlic in butter.
2. Add wine, bring to a simmer.
3. Add mussels, cover and cook until open (5–7 mins).
4. Garnish with parsley and lemon.

Herbed Goat Cheese Crostini

Ingredients:

- Baguette, sliced and toasted
- 1/2 cup goat cheese
- Fresh thyme or rosemary
- Honey drizzle (optional)

Instructions:

1. Mix herbs into goat cheese.
2. Spread on toasted baguette slices.
3. Optional: drizzle with honey for a sweet finish.

Gnocchi with Brown Butter Sage

Ingredients:

- 1 lb gnocchi (fresh or store-bought)
- 3 tbsp butter
- 6 fresh sage leaves
- Grated Parmesan

Instructions:

1. Cook gnocchi until they float.
2. In a skillet, melt butter until golden, add sage.
3. Toss gnocchi in brown butter and finish with Parmesan.

Sweet Potato and Feta Hash

Ingredients:

- 1 large sweet potato, diced
- 1/4 onion, chopped
- 1 tbsp olive oil
- 1/4 cup crumbled feta
- Fresh parsley

Instructions:

1. Sauté sweet potato and onion in olive oil until tender.
2. Add feta and parsley before serving.

Frittata with Spinach and Leeks

Ingredients:

- 6 eggs
- 1 cup spinach
- 1/2 leek, sliced
- 1/4 cup milk
- Olive oil, salt, pepper

Instructions:

1. Sauté leeks in olive oil, add spinach until wilted.
2. Whisk eggs with milk, salt, and pepper.
3. Pour over veggies and cook on low until set.
4. Finish under broiler for golden top.

Lemon Ricotta Pancakes

Ingredients:

- 1 cup ricotta cheese
- 2 eggs
- 1/2 cup flour
- Zest and juice of 1 lemon
- 1 tbsp sugar
- Butter for cooking

Instructions:

1. Mix ricotta, eggs, lemon, sugar, and flour.
2. Cook pancakes in butter until golden on both sides.
3. Serve with syrup or powdered sugar.

Honey Glazed Carrots with Thyme
Ingredients:

- 1 lb carrots, peeled and sliced
- 2 tbsp honey
- 1 tbsp butter
- Fresh thyme sprigs
- Salt and pepper

Instructions:

1. Roast carrots with butter, honey, and thyme at 400°F (200°C) for 20–25 minutes.
2. Toss halfway and roast until caramelized.

Seared Tuna with Sesame Crust

Ingredients:

- 2 tuna steaks
- 2 tbsp sesame seeds (black and white)
- 1 tbsp olive oil
- 1 tbsp soy sauce
- 1 tsp wasabi paste (optional)
- Fresh cilantro (optional)

Instructions:

1. Coat tuna steaks in sesame seeds.
2. Heat olive oil in a pan and sear tuna for 1-2 minutes per side (adjust based on desired doneness).
3. Drizzle with soy sauce and wasabi, garnish with cilantro.

Soft-Boiled Eggs with Toast Soldiers

Ingredients:

- 4 eggs
- 2 slices of bread, toasted
- Salt, pepper

Instructions:

1. Boil eggs for 6-7 minutes for a soft, runny center.
2. Toast bread and cut into strips ("soldiers").
3. Serve eggs in holders, sprinkle with salt and pepper, and dip with toast soldiers.

Maple Dijon Roasted Chicken Thighs

Ingredients:

- 4 bone-in, skin-on chicken thighs
- 2 tbsp maple syrup
- 1 tbsp Dijon mustard
- 1 tbsp olive oil
- Salt, pepper, thyme

Instructions:

1. Preheat oven to 375°F (190°C).
2. Mix maple syrup, Dijon, olive oil, salt, pepper, and thyme.
3. Coat chicken thighs in the marinade and roast for 30-35 minutes.

Balsamic Glazed Portobello Mushrooms

Ingredients:

- 4 large Portobello mushrooms
- 2 tbsp balsamic vinegar
- 1 tbsp olive oil
- 1 tsp honey
- Fresh thyme

Instructions:

1. Preheat oven to 400°F (200°C).
2. Mix balsamic vinegar, olive oil, honey, and thyme.
3. Brush mushrooms with glaze and roast for 15 minutes, flipping halfway.

Pan-Fried Halloumi with Grapes

Ingredients:

- 8 oz halloumi cheese, sliced
- 1 cup red or green grapes, halved
- 1 tbsp olive oil
- 1 tbsp honey
- Fresh mint

Instructions:

1. Heat olive oil in a pan and fry halloumi slices until golden and crispy.
2. In the same pan, heat honey and add grapes, cooking for 2-3 minutes.
3. Serve halloumi with honeyed grapes and garnish with mint.

Roasted Beet and Orange Salad

Ingredients:

- 2 roasted beets, peeled and sliced
- 2 oranges, peeled and segmented
- 2 cups arugula
- 1 tbsp olive oil
- 1 tbsp balsamic vinegar
- Crumbled goat cheese

Instructions:

1. Toss beets, orange segments, and arugula in olive oil and balsamic vinegar.
2. Top with goat cheese before serving.

Creamy Garlic Parmesan Orzo

Ingredients:

- 1 cup orzo pasta
- 2 tbsp butter
- 2 garlic cloves, minced
- 1/2 cup Parmesan cheese
- 1/4 cup cream
- Salt, pepper

Instructions:

1. Cook orzo according to package instructions.
2. Sauté garlic in butter until fragrant, then add cream and Parmesan.
3. Stir in cooked orzo, season with salt and pepper.

Caramelized Onion Tart

Ingredients:

- 1 sheet puff pastry
- 2 large onions, sliced
- 2 tbsp butter
- 1 tbsp brown sugar
- 1 tbsp balsamic vinegar
- 1/4 cup goat cheese (optional)

Instructions:

1. Preheat oven to 400°F (200°C).
2. Sauté onions in butter until soft, add sugar and balsamic, cook until caramelized.
3. Roll out puff pastry, top with onions, and bake for 15-20 minutes.

Herb Crusted Baked Cod

Ingredients:

- 4 cod fillets
- 1/2 cup breadcrumbs
- 1/4 cup Parmesan cheese
- 2 tbsp fresh parsley, chopped
- 1 tbsp lemon zest
- 2 tbsp olive oil

Instructions:

1. Preheat oven to 375°F (190°C).
2. Mix breadcrumbs, Parmesan, parsley, and lemon zest.
3. Coat cod fillets with olive oil and top with breadcrumb mixture.
4. Bake for 12-15 minutes.

Arugula Pear Salad with Blue Cheese

Ingredients:

- 4 cups arugula
- 2 pears, sliced
- 1/4 cup blue cheese crumbles
- 1/4 cup walnuts, toasted
- Balsamic glaze

Instructions:

1. Toss arugula, pear slices, blue cheese, and walnuts.
2. Drizzle with balsamic glaze before serving.

White Wine Garlic Clams

Ingredients:

- 2 lbs fresh clams, scrubbed
- 1 tbsp olive oil
- 4 garlic cloves, minced
- 1/2 cup white wine
- 1 tbsp butter
- Fresh parsley, chopped
- Lemon wedges

Instructions:

1. Heat olive oil in a large pan. Add garlic and cook until fragrant.
2. Add clams and white wine, cover, and cook for 5-7 minutes until clams open.
3. Stir in butter and parsley, serve with lemon wedges.

Shaved Brussels with Lemon and Pecorino

Ingredients:

- 1 lb Brussels sprouts, thinly shaved
- 2 tbsp olive oil
- 1 tbsp lemon juice
- 1/4 cup Pecorino cheese, shaved
- Salt, pepper

Instructions:

1. Toss shaved Brussels sprouts with olive oil, lemon juice, salt, and pepper.
2. Top with Pecorino and serve chilled or at room temperature.

Buttered Leeks and Poached Egg Toast

Ingredients:

- 2 leeks, sliced
- 1 tbsp butter
- 2 eggs
- 2 slices sourdough bread
- Salt, pepper
- Fresh chives (optional)

Instructions:

1. Sauté leeks in butter until tender.
2. Poach eggs and toast bread slices.
3. Top toast with leeks, poached eggs, and garnish with chives.

Roasted Red Pepper Pasta

Ingredients:

- 12 oz pasta (penne or spaghetti)
- 2 roasted red peppers, blended into puree
- 1 tbsp olive oil
- 2 garlic cloves, minced
- 1/4 cup heavy cream
- Fresh basil, chopped
- Parmesan cheese

Instructions:

1. Cook pasta according to package instructions.
2. Sauté garlic in olive oil, add red pepper puree and cream.
3. Toss pasta in sauce, top with basil and Parmesan.

Mushroom Toast with Gruyère

Ingredients:

- 8 oz mushrooms, sliced
- 2 tbsp butter
- 2 slices sourdough bread
- 1/2 cup Gruyère cheese, shredded
- Fresh thyme, chopped
- Salt, pepper

Instructions:

1. Sauté mushrooms in butter until tender.
2. Toast sourdough and top with mushrooms and Gruyère.
3. Bake in the oven at 375°F (190°C) for 5-7 minutes, until cheese is melted.
4. Garnish with thyme.

Baked Sweet Potato with Tahini Drizzle

Ingredients:

- 2 large sweet potatoes
- 2 tbsp tahini
- 1 tbsp lemon juice
- 1 tsp honey
- Salt, pepper
- Fresh parsley

Instructions:

1. Bake sweet potatoes at 400°F (200°C) for 40-45 minutes, until soft.
2. Mix tahini, lemon juice, honey, salt, and pepper.
3. Drizzle over baked sweet potatoes and garnish with parsley.

Mediterranean Chickpea Bowl

Ingredients:

- 1 can (15 oz) chickpeas, drained and rinsed
- 1 cucumber, chopped
- 1 tomato, chopped
- 1/4 red onion, thinly sliced
- 1/4 cup feta cheese, crumbled
- 2 tbsp olive oil
- 1 tbsp lemon juice
- Fresh parsley, chopped
- Salt, pepper

Instructions:

1. Combine chickpeas, cucumber, tomato, onion, and feta in a bowl.
2. Drizzle with olive oil and lemon juice, toss to combine.
3. Garnish with parsley and season with salt and pepper.

Zucchini Fritters with Dill Yogurt

Ingredients:

- 2 medium zucchinis, grated
- 1/4 cup flour
- 1 egg
- 2 tbsp fresh dill, chopped
- 1/2 cup Greek yogurt
- 1 tbsp lemon juice
- Salt, pepper

Instructions:

1. Squeeze excess moisture from zucchini.
2. Mix zucchini with flour, egg, dill, salt, and pepper.
3. Fry in olive oil until golden brown.
4. Serve with Greek yogurt mixed with lemon juice and dill.

Roasted Cauliflower Steak

Ingredients:

- 1 head cauliflower, sliced into steaks
- 2 tbsp olive oil
- 1 tsp paprika
- 1/2 tsp cumin
- Salt, pepper
- Fresh cilantro (optional)

Instructions:

1. Preheat oven to 400°F (200°C).
2. Drizzle cauliflower steaks with olive oil and season with paprika, cumin, salt, and pepper.
3. Roast for 20-25 minutes, flipping halfway, until tender and caramelized.
4. Garnish with cilantro before serving.

Artichoke and Spinach Flatbread

Ingredients:

- 1 flatbread or pizza crust
- 1/2 cup spinach, chopped
- 1/2 cup artichoke hearts, chopped
- 1/4 cup ricotta cheese
- 1/4 cup mozzarella cheese, shredded
- 2 tbsp olive oil
- 1 garlic clove, minced
- Salt, pepper

Instructions:

1. Preheat the oven to 375°F (190°C).
2. Sauté spinach and garlic in olive oil until wilted.
3. Spread ricotta over the flatbread, top with spinach, artichokes, mozzarella, salt, and pepper.
4. Bake for 10-12 minutes until golden and bubbly.

Eggplant Caponata on Sourdough

Ingredients:

- 1 medium eggplant, diced
- 1/2 onion, chopped
- 1 bell pepper, chopped
- 2 tbsp capers
- 1/4 cup balsamic vinegar
- 1/4 cup tomato paste
- 1 tbsp olive oil
- 1 tsp sugar
- 4 slices sourdough bread
- Fresh basil

Instructions:

1. Heat olive oil in a pan and sauté onion, bell pepper, and eggplant until soft.
2. Add capers, balsamic vinegar, tomato paste, and sugar, and simmer for 10 minutes.
3. Toast sourdough slices, top with caponata, and garnish with fresh basil.

Warm Lentil Salad with Dijon Vinaigrette

Ingredients:

- 1 cup cooked lentils
- 1/2 red onion, thinly sliced
- 1/4 cup feta cheese, crumbled
- 1/4 cup fresh parsley, chopped
- 1 tbsp Dijon mustard
- 2 tbsp olive oil
- 1 tbsp red wine vinegar
- Salt, pepper

Instructions:

1. Combine cooked lentils, onion, feta, and parsley in a bowl.
2. Whisk together Dijon mustard, olive oil, red wine vinegar, salt, and pepper.
3. Toss lentils with vinaigrette and serve warm.

Smashed Chickpea Avocado Salad

Ingredients:

- 1 can (15 oz) chickpeas, drained and mashed
- 1 avocado, mashed
- 1/4 cup red onion, chopped
- 1/4 cup cilantro, chopped
- 1 tbsp lime juice
- Salt, pepper

Instructions:

1. In a bowl, mash chickpeas and avocado together.
2. Add red onion, cilantro, lime juice, salt, and pepper.
3. Stir until well combined and serve as a dip or on toast.

Spaghetti Aglio e Olio

Ingredients:

- 12 oz spaghetti
- 4 garlic cloves, thinly sliced
- 1/4 tsp red pepper flakes
- 1/4 cup olive oil
- Fresh parsley, chopped
- Salt, pepper
- Grated Parmesan (optional)

Instructions:

1. Cook spaghetti according to package instructions, reserving 1/2 cup pasta water.
2. In a pan, heat olive oil and sauté garlic until golden. Add red pepper flakes and reserved pasta water.
3. Toss the cooked spaghetti into the garlic oil, season with salt and pepper, and garnish with parsley. Serve with Parmesan if desired.

Greek Yogurt with Honey and Pistachios

Ingredients:

- 1 cup Greek yogurt
- 2 tbsp honey
- 1/4 cup pistachios, chopped
- Fresh mint (optional)

Instructions:

1. Spoon Greek yogurt into a bowl.
2. Drizzle with honey and sprinkle with chopped pistachios.
3. Garnish with fresh mint if desired and serve immediately.

Tomato Confit on Baguette

Ingredients:

- 1 pint cherry tomatoes, halved
- 2 tbsp olive oil
- 2 garlic cloves, smashed
- 1 tsp dried oregano
- 1 baguette, sliced
- Fresh basil, chopped
- Salt, pepper

Instructions:

1. Preheat oven to 350°F (175°C).
2. Place tomatoes, olive oil, garlic, oregano, salt, and pepper on a baking sheet. Roast for 25-30 minutes until tomatoes are soft.
3. Toast baguette slices in the oven for 5 minutes.
4. Spoon tomato confit onto toasted baguette slices and garnish with fresh basil.

Baked Eggs in Marinara
Ingredients:

- 1 cup marinara sauce
- 2 large eggs
- 1 tbsp olive oil
- 1/4 cup grated Parmesan cheese
- Fresh basil, chopped
- Salt, pepper

Instructions:

1. Preheat oven to 375°F (190°C).
2. Spoon marinara sauce into a small baking dish and make two small wells.
3. Crack an egg into each well, drizzle with olive oil, and sprinkle with Parmesan.
4. Bake for 12-15 minutes until eggs are set.
5. Garnish with basil, salt, and pepper, and serve immediately.

Smoked Salmon and Cream Cheese Bagel
Ingredients:

- 2 bagels, halved
- 4 oz cream cheese
- 4 oz smoked salmon
- 1/4 red onion, thinly sliced
- Fresh dill, chopped
- Lemon wedges

Instructions:

1. Toast bagel halves until golden.
2. Spread cream cheese generously on each bagel half.
3. Top with smoked salmon, red onion slices, and fresh dill.
4. Serve with lemon wedges for extra flavor.

Chèvre and Roasted Grape Crostini

Ingredients:

- 1 baguette, sliced
- 1 cup grapes, halved
- 1 tbsp olive oil
- 4 oz chèvre cheese (goat cheese)
- 1 tbsp honey
- Fresh thyme, chopped
- Salt, pepper

Instructions:

1. Preheat oven to 375°F (190°C).
2. Toss grapes in olive oil, salt, and pepper, and roast on a baking sheet for 15-20 minutes.
3. Toast baguette slices in the oven for 5 minutes.
4. Spread chèvre cheese on each toast, top with roasted grapes, drizzle with honey, and garnish with fresh thyme.

Crispy Sage Butter Ravioli

Ingredients:

- 1 package fresh ravioli
- 1/4 cup butter
- 10-12 fresh sage leaves
- 1 tbsp olive oil
- Salt, pepper
- Grated Parmesan cheese

Instructions:

1. Cook ravioli according to package instructions.
2. In a pan, melt butter and olive oil over medium heat. Add sage leaves and cook until crispy (about 2 minutes).
3. Remove sage and set aside.
4. Toss cooked ravioli in the sage butter, season with salt and pepper, and sprinkle with Parmesan.
5. Garnish with crispy sage leaves before serving.